Vladimir Putin The

Everything You Need to Know About Russian President Vladimir Putin

Allen Gessen

TABLE OF CONTENT

INTRODUCTION

Vladimir Putin, full name **Vladimir Vladimirovich Putin** (born October 7, 1952, Leningrad, Russia, USSR [now St. Petersburg, Russia]), Russian intelligence officer and politician who served as President of Russia (1999–2008, 2012–) and was Prime Minister of Russia (1999, 2008–12). For 16 years, he worked as a KGB foreign intelligence officer, rising to the rank of lieutenant colonel (Podpolkovnik) before resigning in 1991 to pursue a political career in Saint Petersburg. In 1996, he relocated to Moscow to join President Boris Yeltsin's administration. Before being appointed Prime Minister in August 1999, he briefly served as Director of the Federal Security Service (FSB) and Secretary of the Security Council. Following Yeltsin's resignation, Putin took over as acting president and was elected president for the first time less than four months later. In 2004, he was re-elected. Because he was constitutionally limited to two consecutive terms as president at the time, Putin served as prime minister again under Dmitry Medvedev from 2008 to 2012. He was re-elected in 2012 in an election marred by allegations of fraud and protests; he was re-elected in 2018. Following a referendum, he signed constitutional amendments into law in April 2021, including one that would allow him to run for reelection twice more, potentially extending his presidency to 2036.

Following economic reforms and a fivefold increase in the price of oil and gas, the Russian economy grew on average by 7% per year during Putin's first term as president. He also led Russia through a war against Chechen separatists, restoring federal control over the territory. Under Medvedev's leadership, he supervised military and police reform, as well as Russia's triumph in the conflict with Georgia.

BIRTH AND EARLY LIFE

Putin was born on October 7, 1952, in Leningrad, Soviet Union (now Saint Petersburg, Russia), to Vladimir Spiridonovich Putin (1911–1999) and Maria Ivanovna Putina (née Shelomova; 1911–1998), the youngest of three children. Spiridon Putin, his grandpa, worked as a personal cook for Vladimir Lenin and Joseph Stalin. [24] [25] Putin's birth was preceded by the deaths of two brothers: Albert, who died in infancy in the 1930s, and Viktor, who died of diphtheria and malnutrition in 1942 during the Nazi Germany-led Siege of Leningrad. [26] [27].

Putin's mother worked in a factory, and his father joined the Soviet Navy as a conscript in the early 1930s, representing the submarine fleet. During World War II, his father was a member of the NKVD's annihilation brigade. [28] [29] [30] He was afterward sent to the regular army, where he was seriously injured in 1942. German occupants of the Tver region executed Putin's maternal grandmother in 1941, and his maternal uncles vanished during World War II on the Eastern Front. Putin began his education at School No. 193 on Baskov Lane, near his home, on September 1, 1960. He was one of only a few students in the class of about 45 who were not yet members of the Young Pioneer organization. He began practicing sambo and judo at the age of 12. In his spare time, he enjoyed reading Karl Marx, Friedrich Engels, and Vladimir Lenin.

Putin studied German at Saint Petersburg High School 281 and is fluent in the language.

He earned a law degree from Leningrad State University named after Andrei Zhdanov (now Saint Petersburg State University) in 1975. His dissertation topic was "The Most Favored Nation Trading Principle in

International Law." He was forced to join the Communist Party of the Soviet Union (CPSU) while there and remained a member until it was dissolved in 1991.

Putin met Anatoly Sobchak, an assistant professor who taught business law and went on to co-author the Russian constitution as well as French corruption schemes. Putin would have an impact on Sobchak's career in Saint Petersburg, and Sobchak would have an impact on Putin's career in Moscow.

PUTINS DAYS AT KGB – THE TRANSITION TO POLITICS

Putin joined the KGB in 1975 and received his training at the 401st KGB school in Okhta, Leningrad. He started his career as a counter-intelligence officer in the Second Chief Directorate before moving to the First Chief Directorate, where he was in charge of monitoring foreigners and consular officials in Leningrad. In September 1984, Putin was sent to Moscow for additional training at the Yuri Andropov Red Banner Institute.

According to multiple reports, Putin was sent by the KGB to New Zealand, where he allegedly worked undercover as a Bata shoe salesman in central Wellington, among other aliases.

From 1985 to 1990, he worked as a translator undercover in Dresden, East Germany.

Unlike Putin's attendance in East Germany, his presence in New Zealand has never been acknowledged by Russian security agencies, but has been substantiated by eyewitness claims and official records in New Zealand. Putin served in both Wellington and Auckland, according to former Waitakere City mayor Bob Harvey and former Prime Minister David Lange in the 1980s.

According to an unidentified former RAF member, militants gave Putin with a list of weaponry during one of these sessions in Dresden, which were later given to the RAF in West Germany. Putin allegedly handled a neo-Nazi, Rainer Sonntag, and attempted to attract an author of a poisons study, according to Klaus Zuchold, who claimed to have been recruited by Putin. [51] Putin and an interpreter reportedly met with Germans to be recruited for wireless communications matters. Due to journeys of German engineers he recruited to South-East Asia and the West, he became involved in wireless communications technologies.

According to Putin's official biography, he saved the files of the Soviet Cultural Center (House of Friendship) and the KGB villa in Dresden for the official authorities of the would-be united Germany to prevent demonstrators, including KGB and Stasi agents, from obtaining and destroying them during the fall of the Berlin Wall on November 9, 1989. He then allegedly burned only the KGB papers in a matter of hours, but saved the Soviet Cultural Center records for German authorities. During the burning, nothing is said regarding the selection criteria, such as about Stasi data or files from other German Democratic Republic or Soviet agencies.

He claimed that a furnace failure in Germany resulted in the abandonment of many papers, but that numerous documents from the KGB home were transferred to Moscow.

Despite the fact that the KGB and the Soviet Army continued to operate in eastern Germany after the Communist East German government fell apart, Putin was forced to quit active KGB employment as a result of questions raised about his loyalty during demonstrations in Dresden and elsewhere. He returned to Leningrad in early 1990 as a member of the "active reserves," and while working on his doctoral dissertation, he worked for three months at Leningrad State University's International Affairs section, reporting to Vice-Rector Yuriy Molchanov.

He kept an eye out for fresh KGB recruits, kept an eye on the student body, and rekindled his acquaintance with his former professor, Anatoly Sobchak, who would soon become Leningrad's Mayor. On the second day of the 1991 Soviet coup d'état attempt against Soviet President Mikhail Gorbachev, Putin claimed to have resigned with the rank of lieutenant colonel. "I instantly determined whose side I was on as soon as the coup began," Putin stated, adding that the decision was difficult because he had spent the majority of his life with "the organs."

In 1999, Putin described communism as "a dead-end, distant from civilization's mainstream."

August 1999

Vladmir Putin is appointed Prime Minister by President Boris Yeltin

December 1999

Yeltin resigns and Vladmir Putin becomes acting President

March 2000

Putin wins the Presidential election

March 2004

Putin wins his second term as President

May 2008

Putin steps down as president after reaching the constitutional limit of two consecutive terms and become Prime minister under his political ally President Dmitry Medvedev

March 2012

Putin wins a third term as President

March 2018

Putin wins a fourth term as President.

July 2020

Constitutional amendments which allow Putin to run for two more terms after 2024 are passed in a nationwide referendum.

HOW PUTINS MOTHER WAS ALMOST BURIED ALIVE FOR BY RUSSIAN SOLDIERS.

Vladimir Putin has been the president of Russia for two decades and is estimated to be worth $200 billion. Due to the following occurrence that occurred during WWII, his entire existence was extremely close to not happening.

Vladimir Putin's father was a Soviet Union soldier who fought in World War II. His name was Vladimir Spiridonovich Putin.

Putin's father returned home from the front lines for a brief respite during the war. When he arrived at the apartment where he lived with his wife, he noticed a stack of dead bodies in the street and troops loading them into a flatback vehicle. As he got closer, he noticed a woman's legs dangling loose and knew it was her from the shoe she wore.

Maria Ivanovna Putina was her name. He dashed towards the heap of bodies, where he discovered his wife's body. Since the bodies were being carried for a mass grave, he demanded that his wife's body be delivered to him for private burial.

The men were arguing because they were not ready to hand over the body to him. The guys eventually yielded, and Putin's father took his wife's corpse into his arms.

His wife was unresponsive but still breathing when he checked the body.

He then took her to the hospital for treatment, where she gradually recovered and was subsequently discharged.

Vladimir Putin was born eight years after this occurrence.

Vladimir Putin speaks passionately about his mother whenever the occasion arises.

Putin is quoted as saying that his mother passed out from famine and was laid to rest alongside bodies, only to wake up barely in time. According to his story, his father was not with his mother during the occurrence. Putin stated that his father was "always on the battlefield" and "didn't have a chance to look for her."

"She was helped by my uncle." He planned to feed her with his own rations. He was once transferred somewhere for a period of time, and she was on the point of hunger. This is not hyperbole. My mother once passed out from hunger. People assumed she had perished and buried her alongside the bodies.

Fortunately, Mama awoke in time and began moaning. She survived by some miracle. She made it through the entire Leningrad blockade. "They didn't let her go until the danger had passed," Putin wrote.

Hilary Clinton learned about this horrifying event from Vladimir Putin himself, and she included it in her book. Hillary Clinton remembered a conversation with Putin during the Siege of Leningrad when his mother was mistakenly supposed to be dead and nursed her back to health in her biography "Hard Choices," published in 2014.

RUSSIA – UKRAINE WAR

After a quick succession of prime ministers, including two with intelligence backgrounds – Yevgeny Primakov and Sergei Stepashin – Putin was nominated to the same office in August 1999, paving the route for his presidency. He received 53 percent of the vote in the presidential election in March 2000.

Because of the public's desire for a more aggressive leader, the new president was able to implement political reforms that reinforced the state, reversed decentralization, and even harmed democratic institutions and press freedom.

Following the Ukrainian Revolution of Dignity in February 2014, the Ukraine-Russia war began, primarily focusing on the status of Crimea and the Donbas, both of which are internationally recognized as part of Ukraine. The first eight years of the conflict were distinguished by the Russian annexation of Crimea (2014) and the war in Donbas (2014–present) between Ukraine and Russian-backed separatists, as well as maritime events, cyberwarfare, and political issues. The conflict escalated significantly on February 24, 2022, when Russia launched a full-scale invasion of Ukraine, following a Russian military build-up on the Russia Ukraine border that began in late 2021.

Pro-Russian unrest developed in regions of Ukraine following the Euromaidan protests and a revolution that resulted in the overthrow of pro-Russian President Viktor Yanukovych in February 2014. In the Ukrainian area of Crimea, Russian soldiers wearing no insignia gained control of important locations and infrastructure, including the Crimean Parliament. Russia held a contentious referendum, with the result that Crimea would join Russia. As a result, Crimea was annexed. Pro-Russian protests in Ukraine's Donbas area erupted in a battle between the Ukrainian military and Russian-backed rebels from the self-proclaimed Donetsk and Luhansk republics in April 2014.

Unidentified Russian military vans crossed the border into the Donetsk region in August 2014. On the one hand, Ukrainian soldiers fought separatists who were mixed in with Russian troops, while Russia tried to hide its role. After several failed peace initiatives, the conflict became a static fight. Russia and Ukraine signed the Minsk II agreements in 2015, but they have yet to be fully implemented due to a number of issues. By 2019, the Ukrainian government had designated 7% of the country as temporarily occupied.

In 2021 and early 2022, Russia significantly increased its military presence along Ukraine's borders. NATO accused Russia of planning an invasion, which the Russian government strongly denied. Russian President Vladimir Putin has called NATO's expansion a threat to his country and has called for Ukraine to be barred from joining the military alliance. He also espoused Russian nationalist sentiments, questioned Ukraine's right to exist, and incorrectly claimed that Ukraine was formed by Soviet Russia. On February 21, 2022, Russia openly recognized the two self-proclaimed separatist governments in the Donbas and sent troops into the region.

Russia invaded Ukraine three days later. Many in the international community have condemned Russia's actions in post-revolutionary Ukraine, accusing it of violating international law and Ukrainian sovereignty. Many countries imposed economic sanctions on Russia, Russian individuals, or Russian companies, particularly after the 2022 invasion.

In the ongoing Russo-Ukrainian War, no formal declaration of war has been issued. When the Kremlin announced the Russian invasion of Ukraine in 2022, it claimed it would be a "special military operation," avoiding a formal declaration of war. The Ukrainian government, however, interpreted the statement as a declaration of war, and many international news outlets reported it as such. While the Ukrainian parliament has labeled Russia a "terrorist state" for its military actions in Ukraine, it has not issued a formal declaration of war on Russia's behalf.

THE LEGACY OF VLADMIR PUTIN

Russian President Vladimir Putin has crafted a political system that is unlike any other in Russian history, combining Soviet customs with triumphs from the Gorbachev and Yeltsin eras, as well as new characteristics. Russia is far more receptive to Western influence now than it was during the Soviet era. The majority of Russian residents are free to travel, and they have access to the Internet, which allows them to access unrestricted information, discussion, and some online organization. Russian residents are today better off economically than they have ever been since the collapse of formal state economic planning and the occurrence of high oil and gas prices. Consumer products are generally available, providing a sense of well-being to the typical person.

Unlike the upheavals of the 1990s, Putin has been able to instill a sense of stability in the political system, earning him immense popularity among his voters. These achievements, however, have been accompanied with a persistent attack on democracy and civil liberties. Putin has returned to some of the Soviet-style tactics to controlling Russia during his eight years in office, particularly the centralization of power. However, in a unique twist, he has given the security services a considerable autonomous role. While the system appears to be solid in the short term, long-term institutionalization is lacking.

Putin's system is notable for the power it grants the Federal Security Service (FSB), the KGB's successor. While the security services played a smaller role under Yeltsin, the FSB is currently the most powerful force in Russian politics. Its agents make up a significant portion of the Kremlin's employees, and they're increasingly in command of key commercial positions in Russia's rapidly developing state-controlled corporate sector. The FSB has established a closed political system that feeds on creating external enemies and pursues an aggressive foreign policy with little outside monitoring.

Putin's political system has rendered elections completely unpredictable. In the 1999 State Duma elections, Putin and his allies faced off against Moscow Mayor Yury Luzhkov and former Prime Minister Yevgeny Primakov. Putin won that battle and, once in power, systematically reduced elections to a process in which the public is given the opportunity to validate decisions already made in the Kremlin. The appointment of Dmitry Medvedev as Putin's successor in March 2008 is simply the most recent milestone in this process. The Kremlin used state resources to ensure Medvedev's election, as it has in previous elections.

Medvedev received substantial attention on state-controlled media networks, and officials applied pressure at work to guarantee that a large number of voters turned out and voted correctly. There was little chance that the outcome and vote totals would not be "right" because the Kremlin has enormous control over Russia's hierarchy of electoral bodies. To be sure, all genuine opposition candidates were eliminated off the ballot, and Medvedev refused to debate the remaining candidates. Because Russia's constitution prohibits presidents from serving more than two terms in a row, Putin chose to give over official power to a ceremonial successor while remaining in office as prime minister. Putin's informal power as prime minister will now supersede the president's formal powers, ostensibly in contravention of Russia's constitution, which vests the majority of power in the president. It remains to be seen how Putin and Medvedev's relationship will play out in practice. All signs currently point to Putin staying at the top of the pyramid, with Medvedev playing a supporting role.

While Putin campaigned on the rule of law, he has presided over a system that is fundamentally lawless.

Politicians and bureaucrats in Russia selectively apply legislation in order to further their own goals.

Individuals, organizations, and corporations that violate the system are eventually probed by tax officials or fire inspectors, who make it impossible for them to continue their operations. The Kremlin, for example, put pressure on Shell by accusing it of breaking Russian environmental law.

CONCLUSION

Ukraine aimed toward deeper integration with Europe in the decades following the dissolution of the Soviet Union in 1991. When pro-Russian Ukrainian President Viktor Yanukovych attempted to reverse the trend in 2014, he was deposed. Vladimir Putin attacked and annexed the Ukrainian independent region of Crimea after losing an ally. He also sparked separatist uprisings in Donetsk and Luhansk, two eastern Ukrainian provinces where pro-Russian forces fought the Ukrainian government for years.

Volodymyr Zelensky was elected president of Ukraine in 2019 with more than 70% of the vote, running on a populist reform program. Putin ordered a troop buildup along Russia's border with Ukraine in 2021, and Russian forces invaded Ukraine in February 2022 after he proclaimed the start of a "special military operation."

When Vladimir Putin was elected president in 1999, Russia's constitution stipulated that he could only serve two terms in a row. As a result, after his second term expired in 2008, he became Prime Minister until returning to the presidency in 2012. On the other hand, Putin drafted a constitutional amendment in January 2020 that would allow him to serve two more terms as president. It was part of a package of changes approved by the Russian legislature and Russian voters in a July 2020 national referendum.

Vladimir Putin has solidified his dominance during the last two decades and projected an image of Russia as a global force to the Russian people. He transformed Russia from a nascent democratic state to an autocratic one, expanded Russian influence in the Middle East, bolstered Russian ties with China, and demonstrated a willingness to use force to achieve his objectives, as evidenced by his annexation of Crimea in 2014 and large-scale invasion of Ukraine in 2022.

Printed in Great Britain
by Amazon

31396443R00020